DO WHAT YOU LIKE

JOBS IF YOU LIKE
History

Don Nardo

San Diego, CA

© 2025 ReferencePoint Press, Inc.
Printed in the United States

For more information, contact:
ReferencePoint Press, Inc.
PO Box 27779
San Diego, CA 92198
www.ReferencePointPress.com

ALL RIGHTS RESERVED.
No part of this work covered by the copyright hereon may be reproduced or used in any form or by any means—graphic, electronic, or mechanical, including photocopying, recording, taping, web distribution, or information storage retrieval systems—without the written permission of the publisher.

LIBRARY OF CONGRESS CATALOGING-IN-PUBLICATION DATA

Names: Nardo, Don, 1947- author.
Title: Jobs if you like history / by Don Nardo.
Description: San Diego, CA : ReferencePoint Press, Inc., 2025. | Series: Do what you like | Includes bibliographical references and index.
Identifiers: LCCN 2024031274 (print) | LCCN 2024031275 (ebook) | ISBN 9781678209827 (library binding) | ISBN 9781678209834 (ebook)
Subjects: LCSH: History--Vocational guidance--Juvenile literature. | Occupations--Juvenile literature. | Professions--Juvenile literature.
Classification: LCC D16.19 .N37 2024 (print) | LCC D16.19 (ebook) | DDC 331.702--dc23/eng/20240812
LC record available at https://lccn.loc.gov/2024031274
LC ebook record available at https://lccn.loc.gov/2024031275

Contents

Introduction: A Passion for History Opens Up Many Options   4

Archaeologist   7

History Teacher   15

Museum Archivist   22

Park Ranger   30

Documentary Filmmaker   38

Librarian   46

Source Notes   54
Interview with a Librarian   57
Other Jobs in History   60
Index   61
Picture Credits   64
About the Author   64

Introduction: A Passion for History Opens Up Many Options

The study of history involves reading and learning about the peoples, nations, customs, and events of the past. Students who have a passion for history are not just rooted in the past, however. They excel at searching for and absorbing large amounts of information. They learn to consider context. They develop the ability to identify and understand connections between ideas and events of the past and of the present. And they become adept at organizing and communicating their findings and ideas to others. "Experience in handling varied data, building critical thinking, enhancing the capacity to understand change," writes Peter N. Stearns, professor of history and provost emeritus at George Mason University, "these remain our building blocks, connecting directly to the kinds of career success that history majors enjoy."[1]

The qualities described by Stearns are highly valued in many different career fields. Professional historians and history teachers might be the most obvious, but they are far from the only options. People who have a passion for history can find satisfaction and success as educators, researchers, writers, editors, information managers, and in many areas of business. They might work as archivists, who organize and preserve large stores of information about history and other subjects, or as researchers for large corporations, medical organizations, newspapers, and websites. Moreover, the need for new members of most of these occupations is steadily growing.

Training One's Mind to Learn from the Past

What makes history lovers good candidates for so many different occupations is the way that studying the events of the past has trained their minds. People with a passion for history tend to develop certain abilities, aptitudes, and skills that makes workers in those jobs successful and valuable. For example, individuals who love history are more often than not adept at solving problems because their readings about history have shown them how people in the past dealt with their own dilemmas. And today, bosses in almost all professions recognize how valuable problem solvers are. After all, thorny issues requiring problem-solving skills inevitably crop up in virtually all occupations.

History lovers also tend to ask a lot of questions and think about possible ways to answer them. Because so many such questions were asked and answered by individuals in prior societies and civilizations, people who enjoy history learn to recognize repeating patterns of ideas and events in the past. And they recognize that logic dictates that such patterns will repeat themselves in the future. This ability to understand why things occurred in the past makes history buffs extremely beneficial to the organizations, businesses, and companies they work for and often makes them highly prized workers.

Still other abilities that history lovers tend to develop are an attention to detail and a capacity for organizing large amounts of information. While reading about past peoples and societies, they frequently learn about particularly fascinating historical episodes and characters. And not surprisingly, those readers often desire to learn even more about these riveting events and figures. As a result, they become talented at tracking down large amounts of information about small, individual topics, much of that data scattered among dozens or hundreds of sources.

Excelling at Essential Skills

The ability to find such specific data and to organize it into manageable summaries—stories with beginnings, middles, and ends—makes these history buffs increasingly skilled at doing research.

Having workers who are history lovers and excel at doing detailed research and deftly organizing the collected data is a huge plus for almost any business or organization. And such skills can be applied to numerous individual jobs as well.

Perhaps the most important of all the skills that history enthusiasts acquire and that makes them good candidates for a wide variety of occupations is their ability to recognize that most of the problems that now plague humanity did not suddenly appear in recent times. Rather, to one degree or another the ideas, beliefs, trends, and mistakes of the past contributed to the creation of today's world. And studying the mistakes of the past can potentially help people today avoid repeating those errors. As the faculty of the history department of the University of Wisconsin–Madison phrases it, today's history lovers show how "studying history helps us understand and grapple with complex questions and dilemmas by examining how the past has shaped (and continues to shape) global, national, and local relationships between societies and people."[2]

Archaeologist

What Does an Archaeologist Do?

Archaeologists are scientists who study the lives, cultures, and behaviors of peoples and societies of the past. The chief way they do so is by digging up and examining the artifacts, or material remains, of those now-extinct civilizations. The science of archaeology also attempts to determine how those cultures exerted various kinds of influences and impacts on modern societies.

Some of the work done by archaeologists can be physically taxing and very slow paced, even tedious. However, according to Charlotte Frearson, an archaeologist at the Institute of Archaeology at University College London, that work is also almost always fascinating and intriguing. And it can even be exciting and memorable. Indeed, she says, some elements of the popular Indiana Jones movies are quite real. Like that fictional archaeologist, real ones often get involved in international travel, adventure, and the exploration of diverse, colorful cultures. As she notes, however, real archaeologists tend not to become involved in the kind of criminal conspiracies and violence those movies depict.

What can fascinate and excite an archaeologist, Frearson continues, is

A Few Facts

Typical Earnings
Average annual earnings of $60,000 to $64,000

Educational Requirements
Most often a master's degree

Personal Qualities
Observational, analytical, and writing skills

Work Settings
Diverse natural settings, labs, offices, classrooms

Future Outlook
Growth rate of about 5 percent through 2032

the chance of finding artifacts that have remained hidden for thousands of years. The original use of such an object, she says, may at first be mysterious and puzzling. But it is part of the archaeologist's job to solve that mystery by figuring out the true nature of an item, "the meaning of which has been lost,"[3] says Frearson.

Sometimes the meaning or use of a newly unearthed artifact can be disturbing and even a little scary to contemplate, says archaeologist Chuck Spencer. As an example, he cites the time he found a strange-looking object while excavating a deserted town in southern Mexico, a place dating back to 300 BCE. Eventually, he deduced that it was a "skull rack" erected by a group of conquerors who attacked the town. "The heads of people who resisted the invasion," Spencer explains, were "placed on the rack by the conquerors as a symbol of terror."[4]

Indiana University of Pennsylvania archaeologist Sarah W. Neusius points out that not all the discoveries archaeologists make are quite so dramatic or gory. Frequently, she says, archaeologists uncover personal items such as combs, tweezers, and other grooming items or kitchen utensils that show how people prepared their food. Yet such artifacts can be combined to paint a captivating picture of a vanished way of life. Since her days as a graduate student, Neusius says she has been "fascinated by archaeology's ability to tell the story of people lost to standard Western history." Archaeology, she adds, "can do so much more than describe and take care of cool artifacts. It was a heady thing to learn that I could contribute to what was known about people who lived thousands of years ago."[5]

A Typical Workday

Fieldwork is a big part of the work of archaeologists. Fieldwork involves surveying sites of past civilizations and digging at those sites in hopes of finding artifacts that will help tell the story of the

> **A Job That Involves a Lot of Digging**
>
> "When you go on a dig, then you can expect to dig! Archaeology is, first and basically, manual labor. The idea is to remove dirt carefully enough that we can tell exactly how things came to be situated as they were and to record it carefully enough that we can reconstruct what happened in the past. We dig carefully because we want to know the context of every find—that's actually the single most important piece of information we are after. Knowing the context of something can make all the difference in how we understand it."
>
> —Archaeologist Andrea M. Berlin
>
> Andrea M. Berlin, "A Career in Archaeology," Archaeological Institute of America, 2024. www.archaeological.org.

people who once lived there. But fieldwork is by no means the only task performed by archaeologists. They also do a lot of historical research to learn what is already known about the society they are studying. In addition, they prepare written documentation of their finds. This includes dating, studying, and analyzing found artifacts. Archaeologists also create computer-generated simulations of places they are excavating to show what those sites originally looked like. In addition, they write reports and articles summarizing their discoveries; confer with colleagues about those findings; and in the case of archaeologists who teach at universities, lecture their students about those and other archaeological discoveries.

No archaeologist does fieldwork plus all of these other diverse duties in a single day, nor usually in a single week or month. There is no typical workday for an archaeologist, therefore. Nevertheless, it is possible to describe a fairly typical workday for a member of the profession who is in the midst of an excavation. Chuck Spencer describes his own fieldwork, saying:

> We usually get up before dawn and have breakfast. Then we . . . divide into teams and start to dig at about 8 a.m. We usually have about six different operations going on at the same time in different areas [of the worksite]. For example, each team of workmen will be mapping where all the objects were found, and making sure everything is bagged and tagged. [Meanwhile] I'm often taking photographs and consulting with the various excavation teams. So we'll work like that until lunchtime. After we eat, we dig again until about 4 p.m. Then we take everything we find to the lab and drive home.[6]

Education and Training

In most cases a person needs at least a master's degree to become an archaeologist. Typically, that means first getting a bachelor's, or four-year, degree and then taking graduate-level classes for one to two more years and writing a master's thesis. A few very prestigious archaeological positions require a PhD, or doctorate. That entails one to two more years of study and ends with writing a book-length thesis called a dissertation. In addition, some positions in the profession demand that the candidate have experience assisting professional archaeologists at a dig or in a lab.

In rare cases someone who wants to become an archaeologist can enter the profession with only a bachelor's degree. However, that person will need to assist one or more archaeologists for several years doing research, lab work, and fieldwork under the watchful eye of his or her supervisors. Such assistants must also take graduate-level classes on and off during those years.

An archaeologist makes notes on the work being done at a temple complex in Luxor, Egypt. Archaeologists are scientists who study the lives, cultures, and behaviors of peoples and societies of the past.

Skills and Personality

Archaeology is a science, and like all the sciences it requires a fairly hefty array of skills. First, members of the profession need to have strong observational abilities. This is because they will be expected to recognize and detect various attributes of a geographical site that might indicate the presence of buried buildings and artifacts. Archaeologists should also have strong analytical and critical-thinking skills to help them interpret the meaning of what has been found. Good communication skills, including the ability to write and lecture clearly, are also a big plus.

Finally, and no less crucial, archaeologists need to have a lot of physical stamina. When doing fieldwork, they may have to walk long distances while carrying equipment and supplies. Moreover, say the editors of the popular employment site Indeed, "When working at an excavation site, an archeologist may need physical agility in order to perform actions such as digging in a squatting position or on unstable ground. . . . They also need stamina for continued physical labor."[7]

Employers and Working Conditions

A relatively large and diverse number of organizations, companies, and individuals tend to hire archaeologists. For instance, both colleges and museums maintain divisions or departments that sponsor archaeological research and digs. The federal government, along with some state and city governments, sometimes hires archaeologists to excavate sites where historical artifacts have recently, and most often unexpectedly, been unearthed. Other hirers of archaeologists include engineering firms, consulting services, and on occasion, private investors.

Once hired, archaeologists can find themselves working in a wide variety of settings, depending on the nature of the work. The geographical sites where archaeologists do fieldwork exist in a dizzying range of physical settings and conditions. Among them are deserts, marshes, prairies, mines and caves, forests and jungles, hillsides and cliff faces, as well as on ocean floors and underneath modern cities and roads. Often, working conditions can be rugged, cramped, and subject to various kinds of extreme weather. Members of the profession also work in offices, laboratories, the basements and exhibit halls of museums, and college classrooms.

Earnings

The pay for archaeological work can vary somewhat, depending on education levels and the kind of work being done. Those with higher degrees generally earn more money. But overall, according to the Bureau of Labor Statistics (BLS) and other agencies and groups that track national employment, the average range of annual earnings for archaeologists in 2023 was $60,000 to $64,000.

> **Useful Information from Trash and Poop?**
>
> "Artifacts are all the physical, tangible objects that we leave behind, including things like buildings, tools, household items, clothing, food remnants, and sometimes even poop. Yes, poop! We call it a *coprolite*, which means 'fossilized dung.' Yes, it kind of sounds like we look at people's trash, and that's actually pretty accurate. Often times, the best artifacts are found in ancient trash piles, or what we like to call *middens*."
>
> —Archaeologist Jones Lefae
>
> Jones Lefae, "My Career in Archaeology 2018: What It's like to Work in Archaeology," Vegerarchy, February 3, 2019. https://vegerarchy.com.

Future Outlook

Fortunately for members of the archaeological profession, those highly specialized workers remain in moderate demand. The BLS predicts that employment opportunities for archaeologists will grow by about 5 percent through 2032. That is roughly the average rate for all occupations. And it means that there will be several hundred openings for new archaeologists each year during that period.

The main reason that demand for archaeologists remains stable now and likely will in the future is that there is no shortage of historical sites worldwide that need excavating. And society as a whole wants them to be explored. Boston University archaeologist Andrea M. Berlin explains why, saying:

> We humans are a curious species, and we are especially curious about . . . our own past, how we came to be who we are. [Also] people are generally fascinated by objects and places from the past. Even though we can't go back in

time, we can get close to the past by visiting an old place or holding an ancient object. [By doing so] we get a feel for the texture and shape of the past, and . . . see it as something real and personal. So I think there will always be people who want to be archaeologists or learn from them.[8]

Find Out More

Archaeological Institute of America (AIA)
www.archaeological.org
Established in 1897, the AIA promotes the work of archaeologists everywhere and educates the public about the importance of archaeology. The AIA website describes different kinds of fieldwork, tells how to apply for grants, and features resources for job seekers, including young people who desire to join the profession.

Society for American Archaeology (SAA)
www.saa.org
The SAA's chief goals are to promote archaeologists' efforts to increase knowledge of past civilizations and to maintain the existing positive image of the profession. The SAA website contains a useful overview of what archaeologists do and provides career information to young people who want to become archaeologists.

Society for Historical Archaeology (SHA)
https://sha.org
The SHA seeks to expand the science of archaeology to include the surviving documents and folklore of past peoples around the world. The SHA website offers news about digs worldwide, information about archaeological publications and conferences, and advice to young people about obtaining college degrees in archaeology.

History Teacher

What Does a History Teacher Do?

History teachers introduce students to general world history, specific historical periods (such as ancient, medieval, and modern history), US history, and the history of individual states. Aspects of history are taught at all grade levels, but teachers who specialize in history are usually found in middle schools, high schools, and colleges and universities. In addition, history teachers practice their profession in both public and private schools.

Some history teachers choose the profession not only because they find history fascinating but also because they enjoy being around and helping young people expand their knowledge. In the words of Katharina Matro, who teaches world history to ninth graders in Bethesda, Maryland, "I discovered in graduate school that I loved teaching and that I was pretty good at it. I loved introducing students to new worlds, texts, and points of view, demonstrating the importance of studying history and helping them become better writers and critical thinkers."[9]

Yet introducing students to history and improving their skills is only part of her mission as a history teacher, Matro explains. She

A Few Facts

Typical Earnings
About $66,000 annually

Educational Requirements
Minimum of a bachelor's degree

Personal Qualities
Love of history, resourcefulness, patience

Work Settings
Classrooms, occasional field trips to historical sites or museums

Future Outlook
Growth rate of 5 percent through 2032

Which College Courses Should a Would-Be History Teacher Take?

"You'll want to find a college or university with a respected history program and a state-approved teacher preparation program. These two programs will allow you to become well-versed in history topics.... When choosing your history courses, you should aim to take classes that cover a wide range of subjects rather than focusing on a specific time or culture. This will give you a baseline for covering multiple history subjects. If you decide later on to teach about a particular time or culture at the high school or university level, you can take more advanced courses as a part of your master's degree."

—Indeed Editorial Team

Indeed Editorial Team, "How to Become a History Teacher," Indeed, March 30, 2023. www.indeed.com.

also seeks to instill in them a love of learning they will carry with them in later life. And in that way her job gives her a great deal of satisfaction. "On a good day," she goes on, "students walk out of my classroom feeling like we have accomplished something and, as a result, they are motivated to continue learning. And when my students exhibit the same thrill at discovering stories from the past that I have felt since high school, I feel like I have made a difference and am exactly where I belong."[10]

Another aspect of teaching history that motivates and animates the most ambitious and dedicated members of the profession is showing the students that they are doing more than just learning facts about history. More importantly, they themselves are part of history. That is how Stephanie Randolph, a middle school history teacher in Enid, Oklahoma, approaches her job. She tells each new group of students, "No matter your career choice, you are going to leave your mark in history. Everyone you come in contact with will remember something about you. What impression will you leave on people?" The reason for this approach, she told an interviewer, is that "I wanted them see their value. I wanted them to see their worth and what they have to bring to the world. What stood out the most to me was that my students have big goals and big dreams."[11]

Another outstanding history instructor, Chicago middle school teacher Lauren S. Brown, takes a similar approach, which she says brings her a lot of joy. "The main reason I love teaching," she states, "is that I love to tap into the growing awareness students have about the bigger world around them. Teaching [history] means teaching kids about how they are connected to the world and how events in the past still influence our beliefs and actions today."[12]

A Typical Workday

History teachers like Matro, Randolph, and Brown, who try to impart to students that the present is shaped by the past, demonstrate an impressive level of dedication to the job. Good history teachers also show their commitment to good teaching by willingly executing the imposing array of tasks that they perform on a daily or weekly basis. First, those teachers must prepare detailed lesson plans that indicate what will be taught each day and how it will be taught. This might include a lecture by the teacher, a group activity by the students, an in-class reading and writing assignment, a film, or perhaps a mix of some or all of those things.

Other regular duties of history teachers include administering and grading quizzes and exams and keeping track of the students' progress in a course. They might also work individually with students who require extra help. They also take part in meetings with other teachers and staff, and sometimes with parents.

Education and Training

Every US state requires public school teachers, including those who teach history, to obtain a minimum of a bachelor's degree. For history teachers, more often than not, that degree can be in history, education, or a combination in which the person majors in one of the two and minors in the other. Whichever of these approaches the person chooses, he or she can expect to get an initial taste of what it is like to run a classroom. This is because most college teacher education programs include a "practice teaching" component. It consists of teaching a class in a nearby school designated by the college and being supervised by that class's actual teacher.

Also, all states mandate that public school teachers be certified (or licensed). Generally, secondary school teachers get certified to teach grades seven through twelve, and elementary school teachers are certified to teach grades one through six. The requirements to become certified differ slightly from state to state. But most often the person must have obtained a bachelor's degree, completed a period of practice teaching, passed a background check, and passed a general test administered by the state in the teacher's chosen subject area—in this case, history.

In contrast, most US private schools are not required to meet state teacher education guidelines. So history teachers in private schools usually do not need to complete the practice teaching component. Nor do they need to become certified. Nevertheless, a majority of private schools do tend to hire secondary school history teachers who have earned a bachelor's degree.

Skills and Personality

Of the diverse skills that effective history teachers either innately possess or learn, perhaps the most crucial is strong communication skills. According to Teacher.org, a website that discusses

> ### Like It or Not, Grading Students Is Part of the Job
>
> "Let's be honest: one of the worst parts of the teaching profession is grading. Good news, then, for middle school teachers. The grading is less onerous in middle school than in high school. My writing assignments [for middle schoolers] were often a paragraph or two, rather than the page or two (or five) that I assigned in high school. Grading a stack of high school history essays is painful and terribly time-consuming. Grading a stack of [middle school] paragraphs on the significance of the Missouri Compromise? Not so bad."
>
> —Chicago middle school teacher Lauren S. Brown
>
> Lauren S. Brown, "Why I Love Teaching Middle School History," MiddleWeb, November 26, 2019. www.middleweb.com.

various approaches to good teaching, "History teachers must be able to communicate effectively with students and their parents. In addition, history teachers should be able to engage students as they present information through multiple [approaches]. A good teacher strives to bring history to life for their students."[13]

Other skills are beneficial for teachers. One is being resourceful and imaginative, which comes in handy when planning how to present information to students. The object is to present it in ways that will both capture their attention and get them to retain the information. Patience is also important. As everyone who has ever attended a school knows, some students are adept at learning, while for others it is difficult. And a good teacher must be patient with and understanding of the ones who are struggling with the material.

The personality of the teacher also comes into play. Sometimes a person is introduced to aspects of history when quite young, and as time goes on that exposure helps shape his or her general outlook on life. In Stephanie Randolph's words, "History really seems to fit well with my personality. My aunt was a history teacher and I grew up with good history teachers who made it interesting. I really loved Oklahoma history and that was my favorite class I took as a student. Once I started college, I knew I wanted to be a teacher and focused more on history."[14]

Working Conditions

School classrooms are the principal work setting of teachers, including those who teach history. On occasion, however, a history teacher might take his or her students to a lecture in the school auditorium. Or the class might go on a field trip to a nearby historical site. In addition, most history teachers do some of their work at home, especially doing lesson plans and grading student exams or research papers.

Employers and Earnings

According to the Bureau of Labor Statistics (BLS) and the online employment and career site Zippia, in 2022–2023 there were a little over 270,000 secondary and elementary history teachers in the United States. That figure included those who worked for the two primary employers of history teachers—public and private schools. A bit over 81 percent taught in public schools, and a little more than 16 percent did so in private schools.

As for earnings, the BLS and other sources of employment information say that, on average, public school history teachers made roughly $66,000 a year in 2022–2023, whereas their private school counterparts made about $61,000 annually. A few scattered school systems in the country paid considerably more. The highest-paid history teachers in the United States, who taught in the schools in Baltimore, Maryland, earned slightly over $82,000 a year.

Future Outlook

The BLS and other leading employment agencies and online sites all agree that the employment of public and private school history teachers will likely remain stable, at a 5 percent growth rate through 2032. Approximately sixty-seven thousand openings for these educators will occur each year during that period. Overall, most of those new teachers will replace colleagues that retire from the profession or leave it for personal reasons.

Find Out More

American Historical Association (AHA)
www.historians.org

The AHA promotes the idea of academic freedom and supports and offers advice about innovative ways to teach history. The AHA website answers the question "Why teach history?" and offers young people advice on how to get an education to become a teacher of history-related subjects.

National Council for History Education (NCHE)
https://ncheteach.org

The NCHE promotes getting an education in history and supports those college graduates who enter the teaching profession. The NCHE website has a career center to help guide students working toward history degrees, information on how to apply for grants, and diverse resources to aid teachers of history-related topics.

National Council for the Social Studies (NCSS)
www.socialstudies.org

The NCSS promotes the work of secondary teachers of history, civics, geography, political science, sociology, and anthropology. The NCSS website provides information on educational opportunities for prospective, as well as experienced, teachers and news about upcoming teacher conferences.

Museum Archivist

What Does a Museum Archivist Do?

In a nutshell, the job of museum archivist is to preserve and safeguard information and items that have historical significance. Typically, archivists organize, verify the authenticity of, and carefully catalogue various historical documents and artifacts. Documents can include legal papers, letters, diaries, maps, and so forth. Artifacts can consist of photographs, artworks, tools, coins, writing implements, and all manner of the personal belongings of historical figures. Michelle Ganz, an archivist at the History Factory in Washington, DC, concisely sums up the job, saying, "We're like librarians but very specialized, and we work with documents rather than books."[15]

In looking at the occupation as a whole, Ganz particularly focuses on the safeguarding aspect of her work. She states, "I like to say that we are the protectors of history and the guardians of the truth. So it is important that we exist to ensure that history does not get changed, especially in the climate that we're seeing nowadays where there's a lot of revisionism happening. Archivists are critical to ensuring that the truth is both protected and made known."[16]

A Few Facts

Typical Earnings
Average of about $60,000 annually

Educational Requirements
Minimum of a bachelor's degree

Personal Qualities
Detail oriented, well organized, good computer skills

Work Settings
Museums; increasingly some work from home

Future Outlook
Growth rate of 10 to 12 percent through 2032

One of the most fascinating aspects of the job is that when new collections of items arrive at the museum, the archivists often do not know what to expect. As they go through the material to organize it, pleasant surprises can arise, points out Sharon Maxwell, an archivist at the UK-based Museum of English Rural Life.

> You never know what you're going to find. It's a bit like Christmas. I always get really excited! Yesterday I came across a First World War diary from 1916 that I wasn't really expecting to find. It's also really nice to see users get excited and have a "eureka moment" in the reading room when you've managed to find something for them that they've been looking for. . . . It helps you see the point of your work.[17]

Another big plus for members of the profession, says Jenn Parent, an archivist at the Museum of Flight in Seattle, Washington, is that they are constantly learning new things and thereby expanding their knowledge base. "I really like continuously learning," she says. And it can be intellectually stimulating, as well as fun, to encounter "material that sparks an interest or moment of 'Wow!' [There are] so many rabbit holes to go down—like did you know Goodyear made a plane out of rubber? Look it up—the Inflatoplane!"[18]

A Typical Workday

On a given day of the week, a museum archivist can be involved in one or more of a fairly wide range of duties and activities. One frequent responsibility is to unpack and inspect new items that arrive at the facility. The next step is often to do some research online or in the museum's own archives on those items that are not clearly marked or the use of which is unclear. If an item is damaged, it must be fixed to the best of the archivist's ability. If the item is a document of some kind, the archivist usually makes digital copies. That way, if for some reason the item is lost or damaged, the copies will constitute proof of its former existence.

Another common duty of an archivist is to make it easy for librarians, historians, writers, and college students, along with ordinary museum visitors, to have access to and study the archived items. As Parent puts it:

> My days can be quite varied based on what I'm up to that day. From answering a photo request about the Aero Spacelines Super Guppy to giving a tour to students . . . to helping relocate an [artifact] in our storage area, it's never dull. But I think my real favorite is simple: being able to successfully guide a researcher and help fulfill their information need, especially when they reach out to me with what they may think is a long shot. I recently had a researcher ask me if it was fun being both useful and magical. A resounding yes![19]

Education and Training

To become a museum archivist, a candidate for that occupation needs a minimum of a bachelor's degree. One approach is to major in archiving, which, depending on the university that offers it, can be called archives and records management, archives and preservation, archival administration, or other similar names. However, many would-be museum archivists choose to major in history or library science. In such cases, the person has the option of minoring in archiving.

Most of the larger, internationally known museums now prefer entry-level archivists to have a master's degree. That means first obtaining a bachelor's degree and then taking classes for one to two more years, plus writing a master's thesis. The most common

> ### Using Social Media
>
> "With digital records and the Internet, what are the archives of the future going to be? . . . Facebook pages are the diaries and scrapbooks of the future and how are we going to look after those? . . . I will use social media to publicize the new things I have catalogued. So things we've maybe had in the stores for years are now hopefully more accessible because they're catalogued. Though it can be difficult to maintain the momentum on social media when you've got so many other things to do but it is a quick way of getting information out there."
>
> —English museum archivist Sharon Maxwell
>
> Quoted in Alison Hilton, "Explore Your Archive: Interview with an Archivist," Museum of English Rural Life, November 18, 2015. https://merl.reading.ac.uk.

approach is to get a bachelor's degree in history or art history and a master's degree in either archiving or history.

Skills and Personality

The job of museum archivists requires several specific skills and abilities. First, they should have an eye for detail. In the words of Anubha Verma, an editor at the popular employment site Indeed, "The work of archivists is highly detail oriented because they process and manage large amounts of materials and records, many of which they store digitally. To ensure accuracy, they remain keenly aware of their performance as they navigate through complex databases."[20]

Other abilities that a museum archivist should have include strong organizational skills, since they must be able to sort through and categorize the materials and records that will end up being digitally stored. And because digital transfers and storage are the

An archivist digitizes valuable historical books. The primary job of museum archivists is preserving and safeguarding information, which can include all sorts of documents and artifacts.

present accepted manner of dealing with huge amounts of data, excellent computer skills are essential to the job. It also helps to have a strong personal interest in history, a quality that makes it easier to continually absorb historical knowledge while on the job.

Working Conditions

For the most part, museum archivists work in the offices, workrooms, and storage facilities designated by their employers. Often, those spaces are in the lower levels of museum buildings. But they are sometimes located in separate structures on the grounds.

Although those traditional settings remain fairly typical, a significant alternate approach began to take effect during and soon after the global COVID-19 pandemic. For several months during the height of the crisis, museums allowed most archivists to work at home if they chose to. And since that time, some of those specialized workers have accomplished at least a portion of their duties from their homes.

Employers and Earnings

According to the Bureau of Labor Statistics (BLS), in 2022–2023 there were approximately ninety-four hundred museum archivists working in the United States. Large museums in urban areas were not their only employers. A small minority of archivists who were trained to organize, store, and preserve historical materials worked in much smaller museums, exhibit halls, and similar facilities in large libraries, national parks, and even a few corporations.

The size of the facility where a museum archivist works can have a bearing on earnings. This is because in most cases large museums in cities tend to take in more money than the smaller ones and as a result can afford to pay their archivists more. The BLS, the government-sponsored online employment site CareerOneStop, and other similar sources estimate that in 2023 the lowest-paid museum archivists made $35,000 to $45,000 per year, whereas the highest-paid ones made $78,000 to $101,000. The average annual pay of members of the profession that year was about $60,000.

Future Outlook

The BLS projects that in the near future, the outlook for people who want to become museum archivists will likely be quite positive. The BLS predicts that the rate of growth of the profession is on track to be at 10 percent and could rise to 12 percent or more through 2032. That is considerably higher than the average growth rate of 4 to 5 percent for all occupations. The BLS and other employment agencies and sites estimate that there will probably be openings for a few thousand more museum archivists each year until 2032.

Working from Home Gives Archivists More Flexibility

"Because of COVID, we have discovered that we can offer archival services in a whole host of ways that we never thought of. . . . We've discovered that we can work from home. . . . So all of a sudden we've gone from, I'm sorry we can't do that [to] what[ever] works for you and it's making archival work a lot better for a lot of us. So, that has been awesome to see and my hope is that we're not going to just go back [to the way we did it before]."

—Washington, DC, archivist Michelle Ganz

Quoted in Raechel C. Woody, "Ask an Archivist: An Interview with Michelle Ganz," *ArchivesAware!* (blog), October 28, 2021. https://archivesaware.archivists.org.

With all those openings, Sharon Maxwell says, young people who enjoy history and who are not sure what occupation to pursue should definitely "think about working with archives. Young people might think they don't want to just deal with paper, but archives cover all different formats, including sound and film." Anyone who wants to get a small taste of what the job is like, she points out, can offer to do a little volunteer work at a local museum. "Volunteering can help you decide whether it's for you."[21]

Find Out More

American Alliance of Museums (AAM)

www.aam-us.org

The mission of the AAM is to connect people to local museums in part by promoting the breadth of learning they can acquire at those institutions. The AAM website offers advice to prospective museum workers, including archivists, on the best colleges to attend and how to find jobs after they have graduated.

International Council on Archives (ICA)

www.ica.org

The ICA promotes the profession of archivists worldwide and explains the most efficient ways to manage archives of all kinds. The ICA website has a large section that tells how young people can become educated in the field of archival preservation, as well as how to become temporary volunteers in museums.

Society of American Archivists (SAA)

www2.archivists.org

The SAA works to establish a code of ethics for archivists, as well as serves as a source of information about the methods archivists employ. The SAA website lists numerous educational opportunities for young people interested in archival work, including information about colleges and online learning programs.

Park Ranger

What Does a Park Ranger Do?

Park rangers work in national parks, at national monuments and historic sites, and at state parks. They have many duties, including maintaining buildings, roads, and trails, as well as monitoring the health of the park's plant and animal life. In addition, some rangers specialize in historical research and presentation. They are often referred to informally as park guides and public historians. Their job is to lecture park visitors—singly or in groups—about the history of the park.

Park rangers who double as public historians are not necessarily academically trained historians, but they are usually very knowledgeable about the park's history and wildlife. As described by the staff of National Parks Traveler:

> The Park Service historian is the keeper of the essence of American history. Unlike the academic historian who spends his life in the classroom and . . . spends his time in lectures and reading history to classes of undergraduate students, the Park Service historian meets the Ameri-

A Few Facts

Typical Earnings
Average of $50,000 per year for entry level

Educational Requirements
Bachelor's degree

Personal Qualities
Strong organizational and interpersonal abilities

Work Settings
Widely diverse, from cities to remote mountains

Future Outlook
Growth rate of 7 percent through 2030

can people every day. Their audience is the nation. They are the ultimate student of history. They read all of the significant literature pertaining to their subject, and also walk the ground where it occurred. . . . The Park Service historian is not only a teacher and interpreter, but also the best subject matter specialist on the history of his park.[22]

These park rangers who teach the public about history tend to find their jobs highly fulfilling. One of their number is Allison Horrocks, a park ranger and public historian at the Blackstone River Valley National Historical Park, which straddles the border between Rhode Island and Massachusetts. She not only feels that her occupation is important to the public but also enjoys being able to expand her own intellectual horizons while on the job. She says, "I feel lucky that I can explore topics that call to me and ignite my personal interest. I also do my best to use the tangible skills I've honed in service of meaningful projects. . . . For me, being a historian or being a scholar means standing in awe of the human pursuit and love of learning."[23]

A Typical Workday

As might be expected, much of a park-based public historian's time is spent working with visitors. In parks and national monuments that have on-site museums, these specialized rangers may lead the visitors through those facilities, answering questions and expounding on the background and significance of various exhibits. They also often guide visitors around the park or monument, offering insights about the site's place in history along the way.

Those same rangers often have other duties, many of them connected to the historical research the job entails. In Horrocks's words:

Every single week is different for me, and that's a big part of why I like what I do for a living. Most days, I do some kind of "frontline" museum work. This may include giving a tour or working with visitors in some other way. . . . In addition to working directly with visitors . . . I have periods where I am doing more "behind-the-scenes" or planning work. This might entail conducting research or visiting with community partners. . . . I also have desk work—answering emails, keeping track of paperwork, and making plans for the future.[24]

Education and Training

According to the Bureau of Labor Statistics (BLS), Indeed, and other sources that track national employment data, in most cases a candidate for the position of park ranger requires a bachelor's, or four-year, degree. One point in the would-be ranger's favor is that he or she can pick from a wide range of college majors. With occasional exceptions, all will make the candidate hirable by most state and national parks. Three of the most common majors chosen by high school graduates who hope to become park rangers are parks and recreation management, wildlife and forestry, and environmental science. Also popular are ecology and earth science.

For young people who early on aim to specialize in the public historian role in state parks or national parks and monuments, employment experts recommend majoring in history, museum science, or a similar program. Many of the ranger candidates who take this route tend to minor in areas such as ecology, earth science, or parks and recreation management. Park managers who are hiring tend to view such applicants as well rounded.

It is also highly recommended that while would-be rangers are earning their bachelor's degree, they do whatever volunteer work they can. It is common, for instance, for students to spend

> **Teaching and Learning**
>
> "I . . . do a lot of field trips with local students . . . and teach about the geological formation process that has shaped the coastline. Then we head over to our rocky coast. That's where I like to explore the tidepool areas, . . . which are great places to go explore with your family and look for animals that call the shoreline home. . . . What is great is that I get to teach about a lot of different things . . . so it's a great learning experience, the job. I'm always learning every year."
>
> —Acadia National Park ranger Lisa Gerardin
>
> Quoted in Clara Timmons, "An Interview with Ranger Lisa from Acadia National Park," National Park Trust, 2024. https://parktrust.org.

part or all of their summer hiatus from college doing volunteer work at a state or national park. On the one hand, this approach exposes individuals to the career they seek to eventually pursue. A college student who wants to be a park-based public historian may even get to practice lecturing park guests while volunteering. On the other hand, any and all volunteer work will enhance a candidate's résumé later, when he or she formally applies for a job at a park.

Skills and Personality

Certain skills are particularly helpful for individuals who aim to become public historians in state parks or national parks and monuments. Besides a general love of history, one of the most important skills is an aptitude for research. This is because a park ranger who lectures visitors about history needs to read many books and articles about a given historical period or series of historical events. And he or she must be able to retain large portions of that material. In addition, that mass of facts needs to be organized, trimmed, and arranged so that it forms an accurate, informative, and entertaining story.

In order to present that story effectively, the ranger in question should also possess strong interpersonal and oral communication skills. Moreover, having a positive, appealing personality helps a lot. Such attributes will ensure that he or she presents the historical facts in a way that is both fascinating and memorable for the visitors.

Employers and Working Conditions

The places where park-based public historians work include a fairly wide variety of settings. This includes national parks, national monuments, and national historic sites. It also includes state parks and state historic sites. Park rangers who double as public historians might work at urban sites, like the Statue of Liberty in New York Harbor, or in large wilderness areas, such as Yellowstone National Park in Wyoming. They also work in diverse environments, such as Mammoth Cave National Park in Kentucky, Point Reyes National Seashore in California, Gettysburg National Military Park in Pennsylvania, and Haleakala National Park in Hawaii.

The conditions in these locales vary widely. This is partly because some are in well-traveled, easy-to-reach areas, whereas others are in distant, isolated spots far from civilization. Also, in some parks weather is a major factor. The South Rim of Grand Canyon National Park in Arizona, for example, can range from swelteringly hot in summer to freezing and snow-covered in winter. Similarly, park rangers around the country must adjust to all sorts of weather extremes.

Earnings

According to Indeed and other employment sources, the salaries of park rangers vary according to factors such as the park's

A park ranger talks with visitors about the historical significance of the Castillo de San Marcos National Monument in Florida. Park rangers who specialize in historical research lead talks for people who want to learn more about the site they are visiting.

location, how long a person has been doing the job, how many months per year he or she works, and the number and kinds of responsibilities the person has. According to Indeed and some other noted sources of employment data, in 2022–2023 entry-level, full-time rangers made an average of about $50,000 annually. In comparison, earnings were higher for senior park rangers. And the few in major supervisory positions made an average of $110,000 a year.

Future Outlook

The estimated employment outlook for park rangers in the United States in the near future is positive. According to various expert sources, including the BLS and Unity Environmental University in New Gloucester, Maine, in 2022–2023 there were roughly

Explaining Turning Points in US History

"The National Park Service preserves the key turning points in American history. At Independence National Historical Park, visitors learn how the 13 colonies changed and evolved into an independent nation based on the principles written in the Declaration of Independence. . . . At Brown v. Board of Education National Historic Site, the visitor learns how America finally came together with the promise of equality embodied in the Declaration and the Constitution and outlawed the practice of segregation. . . . Similar lessons are learned from our many other parks."

—National Parks Traveler staff

National Parks Traveler staff, "The Role of the Historian in the National Park Service," National Parks Traveler, September 15, 2019. www.nationalparks traveler.org.

thirty-nine thousand park rangers in the country. That number is expected to grow at a rate of about 7 percent through 2030. Counting new rangers hired and figuring in those who will retire during that period, there will likely be close to forty-two thousand US park rangers in 2030.

Find Out More

Association of National Park Rangers (ANPR)
www.anpr.org

The mission of the ANPR is to promote the image and goals of the National Park Service and its rangers. The ANPR website tells young people how to find open positions in various parks; there is also a section on helping find children who have become lost in the larger parks.

National Recreation and Park Association (NRPA)

www.nrpa.org

The NRPA seeks to create communities that feature many parks and recreation facilities that enhance health and well-being. The NRPA website contains extensive information about how young people can work toward careers in public parks; which colleges offer degrees in park management, conservation, and so forth; and where to get still more training.

Park Law Enforcement Association (PLEA)

https://plea43.wildapricot.org

PLEA's overall goal is to facilitate and improve law enforcement in and the protection of visitors to local, state, and national parks in the United States. The PLEA website features information about schools for rangers and how young people can obtain scholarships to those schools.

Documentary Filmmaker

What Does a Documentary Filmmaker Do?

Documentary filmmakers make nonfiction films. Shown on television, in movie theaters, or both, such films deal with real-life events, experiences, and people, either past or present. In a very real sense, film documentaries are historical documents. They tell a true story, and while informing and entertaining TV or movie audiences, they record that story for posterity. Therefore, a documentary filmmaker is a kind of historian.

Some documentary filmmakers are mainly film producers, who hire and pay film crews, including directors, cinematographers, sound technicians, grips, and so forth. Other documentary filmmakers are directors or producer-directors. And a few actually operate the cameras themselves while also producing and directing.

Most documentary filmmakers desire to do even more than create visual historical records and educate and entertain audiences. There is often a hope that one's documentary will contribute to social, political, or other change and

A Few Facts

Typical Earnings
Pay varies widely, depending on experience and reputation

Educational Requirements
None, but bachelor's degree in filmmaking recommended

Personal Qualities
Well organized, adaptable to change, creative, good storyteller

Work Settings
From homes and offices to all manner of outside locales

Future Outlook
Growth rate of 7 percent through 2032*

*This number applies to producers and directors, a group that includes documentary filmmakers.

thereby make humanity's lot better in some way. A truly dedicated film documentarian, American writer Gus Mollasis points out, "embodies a curious spirit to explore and get involved in the fabric of [people's] lives, with a noble goal that while doing so [that person] will leave his or her mark and the world in better shape than before he or she got here."[25]

One well-known documentary filmmaker who hopes to alter human or social behavior that way is Rory Kennedy, who created the celebrated documentary films *Ghosts of Abu Ghraib* and *The Synanon Fix*. "I think the great thing with documentaries," she says,

> is that you can have a sense of compassion and understanding of people or stories or situations that might be foreign to you and that you might not experience in your own life. And I think that is especially important in this day and age when there is such divisiveness in our country and there is a lack of understanding of how people are feeling on the other side. I think that documentaries can help bridge those gaps. It can show why somebody does what they do and [has] the story that they have. I think it can really teach—if you want me to be literal—compassion.[26]

A Typical Workday

As Kennedy and other documentary filmmakers will attest, it is close to impossible to describe a typical day for members of their profession. Indeed, the duties they perform from day to day and week to week are highly varied. They depend on factors such as the documentarian's exact role in the project, the size of the production, and the number of other crew members involved.

Combining Diverse Cinematic Elements

"What the style is [that] I've tried to do is engage these elements I have [at my disposal]: interviews, live cinematography, newsreel footage and still photographs, plus on the oral track: third-person narration, first-person voices, complicated sound effects, and period music. And meld these eight elements in different quantities and amounts for the different films [I've done] . . . into something that people [who watch documentaries] recognize . . . [as] a Ken Burns film. . . . And that I'm happy about."

—Renowned documentary filmmaker Ken Burns

Quoted in Scout Life, "BL's Interview with Documentary Moviemaker Ken Burns," 2024. https://scoutlife.org.

As in other kinds of filmmaking, the duties and activities are usually divided into three principal phases. The first phase is pre-production. During this phase, the documentarian comes up with the initial concept, secures any needed funding, writes or hires someone to write the script, plans ahead for shooting dates and locations, lines up people who may be interviewed in the film, and hires the members of the film crew.

The second phase is production. During this phase, the documentarian oversees the actual making of the film. This can include directing the action and operating the camera. The filmmaker also typically coordinates the locations where filming will take place and reviews each day's footage to ensure quality.

The third and last phase is postproduction. During this phase, the documentarian assembles all the footage and either edits it or supervises a professional editor. He or she also adds or hires professionals to add special visual and sound effects, narration, music, and titles. The filmmaker also typically arranges for any public showings of the finished film.

Education and Training

There is no universal educational prerequisite for becoming a film documentarian. To make documentary films, a person technically does not even need a high school diploma. However, considering the many skills needed for this occupation and the enormous competition among documentary filmmakers, it is extremely difficult to break into the business and even harder to achieve success. So employment experts highly recommend at least obtaining a bachelor's degree in film production.

A few dozen US colleges and universities have respected film departments. Among them are those at New York University, Boston University, and the University of Southern California (in Los Angeles). Such schools allow film majors to gain experience in basic film production techniques, knowledge and practice that will pay off later when they attempt to make professional documentaries.

Would-be film documentarians should also keep up with and closely observe the leading documentaries made by professionals each year. A newcomer should, whenever possible, also keep up with what is happening behind the scenes in the documentary film industry. This will give her or him an idea of who is successful at a given moment in time and why, information that can help guide a newcomer's approach to the industry. Successful film documentarians add that it is a good idea for newcomers to practice by making some sample short films. Even if "made on a shoestring" (filmmakers' lingo for very low-budget), if done competently, these can be shown to potential financial backers.

Skills and Personality

Successful documentary filmmakers usually possess a unique array of skills, some technical and others personal. From a technical standpoint a documentarian needs to know a great deal about the filmmaking process, including all the major steps in preproduction, production, and postproduction. And on a personal level, he or she should be well organized.

Documentary filmmaker Shannon Walsh, creator of *Illusions of Control* and *The Gig Is Up*, believes that people who do what she does should have what she refers to as aliveness and awareness. "Aliveness," she explains, "is about being awake, sensitive, receptive, and embodied. Awareness is about being conscious, sentient, perceptive, and humble."[27]

In particular, Walsh says, a film documentarian must be highly adaptable. Some of the complex circumstances surrounding the making of a film "can change quickly," she points out,

> and being able to pivot and adjust is so often crucial to telling the story effectively. . . . During one of my shoots, our lead character was fighting for justice after her close friend was injured at work and hospitalized. The shoot was planned around capturing an emotionally significant scene when she visited her friend in the hospital. Unbeknownst to the crew on the ground, the hospital did not grant access to our film crew. We had to adapt quickly to the unforeseen circumstance of not being able to access the location for our shoot. Our shot lists and preparation had been centered on this hospital visit, but we had to come up with an alternative approach to telling the story.[28]

Working Conditions

A documentary filmmaker's work settings can vary appreciably, depending on diverse factors. Script writing and other aspects of preproduction typically happen in the homes of the producer, writer, director, or some combination of these. The production phase—in which the actual filming takes place—often finds the

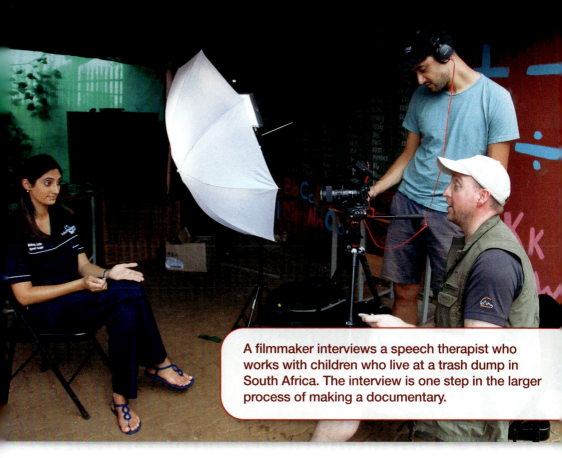

A filmmaker interviews a speech therapist who works with children who live at a trash dump in South Africa. The interview is one step in the larger process of making a documentary.

documentarian and crew in a variety of outside locales, from city streets, to seashores, to forests, to war zones, and so forth. Later, postproduction activities tend to happen mostly indoors, in film and recording studios, offices, and homes.

Employers and Earnings

Most often, employment for a documentary filmmaker occurs in one of two ways. One is when a person, an organization, or a government agency hires the person to make a documentary film. In a case like that, the filmmaker signs a contract, agreeing to do the project for a set amount of money. The amounts vary widely, depending on the size of the project, how long it takes to complete, and the expertise and reputation of the documentarian. If the filmmaker has limited experience, the respected online employment site Indeed states, he or she might make roughly

Capturing Moments in Time

"Documentaries can serve as a means of capturing and archiving some element of the world that we find significance in, and of drawing others' attention to it. There may be something undergoing change, like a neighborhood, that one feels inspired to document as a way of preserving its memory or as a way of contesting or celebrating that change. Stories of the past can be difficult to tell, but these too may be things that we would like to create a record of before they disappear."

—Documentary filmmaker Shannon Walsh

Shannon Walsh, "Skills, Desires, and Dispositions of a Documentary Filmmaker," *POV Magazine*, December 15, 2023. https://povmagazine.com.

the national average salary for a general filmmaker—equivalent to about $42,000 per year in 2022–2023. In contrast, veteran or award-winning documentarians can command two, three, or four times as much for doing the same job.

The second most common employment scenario for a documentary filmmaker is when he or she is the producer and therefore self-employed. In such a case the filmmaker receives most or all of the profits the film generates, which can vary from modest to substantial. If the documentarian is famous and an award winner—like Ken Burns or Rory Kennedy—profits can range into the hundreds of thousands or millions of dollars per film.

Future Outlook

The Bureau of Labor Statistics predicts a 7 percent job growth through 2032 for producers and directors, a group that includes documentary filmmakers. That is considered faster than the average growth rate for all occupations. The main reason for this expected growth is that streaming services and other similar entertainment outlets continue to multiply, creating increased consumer demand for various kinds of film genres, including documentaries.

Find Out More

International Documentary Association (IDA)
www.documentary.org
The IDA supports film documentarians of all nationalities, races, and backgrounds and when possible provides them with needed resources. The IDA website explains how the association helps students and other young filmmakers get grants and fellowships to fund their documentary projects.

Sundance Institute Documentary Film Program (DFP)
www.sundance.org/programs/documentary-film
A department of the renowned Sundance Film Festival, the DFP supports and promotes the work of documentary filmmakers worldwide. Its website provides a good deal of information on how young filmmakers can obtain fellowships and grants to help them create their first film projects and get them seen.

Working Films
www.workingfilms.org
A branch of the famed MacArthur Foundation, Working Films provides funding to young and first-time filmmakers to create documentaries that advance social justice and environmental protection. The group's website tells how interested young people and first-time filmmakers can go about obtaining that funding.

Librarian

What Does a Librarian Do?

The job of the typical librarian once consisted mostly of ordering new books, collecting donated ones, cataloging and shelving those volumes, and lending them out to members in the community. Many librarians still do those things, but as the American Library Association (ALA) explains, "These days a librarian does a lot more than check out materials and shelve books. Technology expert, information detective, literacy expert, [and] community programming coordinator are just a few of the hats a public librarian wears."[29]

The ALA's description of a librarian as an "information detective" comes close to capturing the essential core of the modern occupation of librarian. In fact, librarians are, more than anything else, information professionals and specialists. They are experts in doing complex, expansive research. Sometimes they do research for patrons who request it. Often, they teach people (students as well as adults) how to do their own research, both in the library and on the internet.

According to the ALA, there are more than 120,000 libraries in the United States. By far the larg-

A Few Facts

Typical Earnings
Average of about $64,000 a year in 2023

Educational Requirements
Most often a master's degree

Personal Qualities
Good communication and computer skills, flexibility

Work Settings
Libraries in towns, schools, hospitals, law firms, and more

Future Outlook
Growth rate of 3 percent through 2032

est number are school libraries. Public libraries are the next largest group. Other libraries are found in universities, museums, law firms, hospitals, and scientific institutions and labs. In addition, small libraries of various kinds are maintained by some corporations, churches and synagogues, symphony orchestras, and branches of the US military.

All of these diverse types of libraries are staffed by librarians who possess abilities and skills appropriate to the subjects of the materials stored in those facilities. What they all have in common is the ability to sort and organize a lot of information; seek out reliable, accurate, and sometimes obscure sources for researching a variety of topics; and in some instances, teach others how to do the same. These are the skills people who like history develop, and they are the skills that lie at the heart of the work done by librarians, regardless of the kind of library that employs them.

Typical Workdays

A typical workday or workweek for librarians can vary, often depending on the kind of library they work in. In traditional town libraries, in addition to checking out books for patrons, librarians may update the library's website and do research for patrons. A librarian may also read reviews of new books to help determine whether the facility should purchase those volumes.

In more specialized libraries, the librarians often spend large portions of their time attending to duties directly connected to whatever the areas of specialty may be. The Rock & Roll Hall of Fame in Cleveland, Ohio, has its own library. The library has two different collections, explains librarian Laura Maidens. It has "a library collection and an archival collection. The library materials are published, mainstream materials, like books, DVDs and CDs, and periodicals and magazines. And the archival materials are one-of-a-kind items, like correspondences, recording contracts, photographs, items of that nature," she says. In her job, she oversees

Creating Programs for Their Community

"We created a mindfulness program. We made kits to check out on various related topics (meditation, gardening, yoga, bird watching, sound healing, creative healing, chakras), created a meditation room, held empowered breathing and meditation classes, started an adopt-a-plant program, and got exercise bikes in the library."

—Librarian Katherine

"I worked on an outreach project called Music and Memory that targeted seniors with dementia and Alzheimer's. We would curate a specific playlist for the patrons based on their favorite artists, songs, or music from special moments in their lives."

—Librarian Amanda

Quoted in Adrianna Rebolini, "Here's What It's Really like to Be a Librarian," BuzzFeed News, November 17, 2018. www.buzzfeednews.com.

---

the library materials collection. Maidens explains, "I select what we purchase; I go through requests and suggestions from the staff about things to add to our collection."[30]

The Rock & Roll Hall of Fame librarians also spend considerable time researching and locating artifacts that belonged to famous rock musicians. These objects sometimes end up being displayed in the museum. Also, says Maidens, she and a colleague frequently do extensive research on the lives and contributions of singers and musicians who have been nominated to the hall of fame. Another duty that has become common among librarians, especially those who work for public and school libraries but also in some specialty libraries, is organizing creative in-house educational presentations for the public. The more successful ones combine aspects of knowledge—such as the arts, music, science, medicine, law and justice, and so forth—with elements of entertainment in order to advance learning in local communities. Particularly popular, for example, was a program that was repeated in several of the libraries in the town of Barnstable, Massachusetts, from 2010 to 2020. It featured a local patron who had years before been a professional actor and makeup artist. In a room packed with students from local schools, he did a complex theatrical makeup, changing himself into Quasimodo, the title character of French novelist Victor Hugo's great book *The Hunchback of Notre-Dame*. During the transformation, he talked about the book and its characters, as well as explained the makeup techniques he was using. There was also an emphasis on the history of Notre-Dame Cathedral—when and how it was built and its use as a place of worship over many centuries.

Education and Training

Most libraries today, particularly large ones in cities and on college campuses, require that prospective librarians have a master's degree. The bachelor's degree that the person gets before tackling the master's degree can be in any of a wide variety of disciplines, including history. But for the master's itself, a majority of libraries prefer that it be a master of library and information science degree. Moreover, the college or university the person attends to get the master's degree should be accredited by the ALA.

Skills and Personality

Besides their skills in doing research and organizing large amounts of information, librarians benefit greatly from the ability to communicate well. They consistently speak with patrons and other librarians in person and over the phone. So speaking clearly in a casual, confident, and friendly manner is important to achieve success in the job.

Various tech-related aptitudes and skills, particularly computer literacy, are also required by modern librarians. This is because in today's increasingly online world, librarians use computers for a variety of reasons daily. According to the Bureau of Labor Statistics (BLS), "New information, technology, and resources constantly change librarians' and library media specialists' duties. Workers must be able and willing to continually update their knowledge of these changes to be effective at their jobs."[31]

Employers and Work Settings

Librarians work for a wide variety of employers, among them towns and cities, schools and universities, medical and scientific institutions, military organizations, and several departments of the federal government. For the most part, librarians work indoors, although, weather permitting, they sometimes venture outside to run book sales, oversee educational presentations, take schoolchildren on tours of the library grounds, and so forth.

Challenges of the Job

"[Question:] What challenges, if any, do you and your staff face on a daily basis?

"[Answer:] Having titles available for patrons—needing more of every format for titles; needing the money and ability to keep up with the demand. One big challenge for librarians is having all of the formats patrons want, when they want it. I would love to see a digital copy available alongside every physical copy when checked out—so patrons would be allowed access [to the information] in whatever way they preferred. This is my biggest frustration as a library user as well as a librarian."

—Librarian Jane Martin

Quoted in Smore, "Librarian Interview: Public Library Management with Jane Martin." https://secure.smore.com.

A university librarian assists a student with a project. Librarians are expert at doing complex, expansive research. They also teach others how to do their own research using books, online tools, and other resources.

Earnings

According to the BLS, the median yearly salary for general librarians in the United States in 2023 was about $64,000. That means that half of them earned more than that amount and half earned less. The lowest-paid 10 percent of US librarians made roughly $39,000 that year, and the highest-paid 10 percent made about $102,000. The BLS, Indeed, and other sources of employment information also point out that location can be a factor in salaries for librarians. In many cases those who work at large libraries in metropolitan areas such as New York City, Chicago, Phoenix, Atlanta, Boston, and Los Angeles tend to make more money than those who work at small libraries in more rural areas.

Future Outlook

As reported by the BLS and other sources, the immediate future for librarians is stable and expected to stay that way for a long time to come. The BLS states that there were slightly more than 141,000 working librarians in the United States in 2022–2023. The profession is expected to grow at a rate of about 3 percent through 2032 and very possibly several years beyond that. That growth rate is roughly the same as the average growth rate for all occupations in the country combined.

Moreover, employment experts point out that the often-heard rumor that books are in rapid decline (thanks to the internet) and that the need for libraries is decreasing is false. In the words of a librarian who identified herself simply as Karrah in an online interview:

> In our post-truth world, libraries are more important than ever. Where else can anyone, regardless of their socioeconomic standing, access the information so critical to navigating our digital world? The library is a place that ANYONE can come and visit, whether that be for 10 minutes or the whole day, and not have to buy a cup of coffee. If you believe in democracy, go sign up for a library card.[32]

Find Out More

American Library Association (ALA)
www.ala.org
The ALA is the premier professional organization for librarians in the United States. Its mission is to promote librarians' work and encourage their ongoing excellence. The ALA website contains extensive information for aspiring librarians on grants, scholarships, online classes, and much more.

Council on Library & Information Resources (CLIR)

www.clir.org

CLIR promotes teaching, research, and learning among librarians and other individuals who work for institutions where learning takes place. Its website provides several links to information about how students and others interested in becoming librarians can obtain fellowships and grants to further their studies.

Special Libraries Association (SLA)

https://sla.org

Established in 1909, the SLA is a worldwide organization that promotes the work of librarians in specialized settings such as corporations, law firms, and hospitals. The SLA website contains information and advice on how aspiring librarians can get their careers going.

Source Notes

Introduction: A Passion for History Opens Up Many Options

1. Peter N. Stearns, "Why Study History? Revisited," Perspectives on History, September 18, 2020. www.historians.org.
2. University of Wisconsin–Madison, "Why Should You Study History?" https://history.wisc.edu.

Archaeologist

3. Quoted in Ilana Kowarki, "What Archaeology Is and How to Become an Archaeologist," U.S. News & World Report, October 22, 2020. www.usnews.com.
4. Chuck Spencer, "Being an Archaeologist," American Museum of Natural History. www.amnh.org.
5. Sarah W. Neusius, "How I Became an Archaeologist," Carnegie Museum of Natural History, 2020. https://carnegiemnh.org.
6. Spencer, "Being an Archaeologist."
7. Indeed Editorial team, "What Is an Archaeologist? (Job Duties and How to Become One)," Indeed, November 17, 2022. www.indeed.com.
8. Andrea M. Berlin, "A Career in Archaeology," Archaeological Institute of America, 2024. www.archaeological.org.

History Teacher

9. Katharina Matro, "For the Love of Teaching," American Historical Association, January 1, 2018. www.historians.org.
10. Matro, "For the Love of Teaching."
11. Quoted in Jennifer Kisling, "Inspiring Students to Leave Their Mark on History," I Love Teaching (blog), July 30, 2020. https://iloveteaching.blog.
12. Lauren S. Brown, "Why I Love Teaching Middle School History," MiddleWeb, November 26, 2019. www.middleweb.com.

13. Teacher.org, "How to Become a History Teacher," 2024. www.teacher.org.
14. Quoted in Kisling, "Inspiring Students to Leave Their Mark on History."

Museum Archivist

15. Quoted in Rachael C. Woody, "Ask an Archivist: An Interview with Michelle Ganz," *ArchivesAware!* (blog), October 28, 2021. https://archivesaware.archivists.org.
16. Quoted in Woody, "Ask an Archivist."
17. Quoted in Alison Hilton, "Explore Your Archive: Interview with an Archivist," Museum of English Rural Life, November 18, 2015. https://merl.reading.ac.uk.
18. Quoted in Anna Trammell, "There's an Archivist for That! Interview with Jenn Parent, Reference Archivist, the Museum of Flight," *ArchivesAware!* (blog), October 8, 2019. https://archivesaware.archivists.org.
19. Quoted in Trammell, "There's an Archivist for That!"
20. Anubha Verma, "What Is an Archivist and What Do They Do?," Indeed, July 25, 2023. www.indeed.com.
21. Quoted in Hilton, "Explore Your Archive."

Park Ranger

22. National Parks Traveler staff, "The Role of the Historian in the National Park Service," National Parks Traveler, September 15, 2019. www.nationalparkstraveler.org.
23. Quoted in *Contingent Magazine*, "How Allison Horrocks Does History," February 9, 2022. https://contingentmagazine.org.
24. Quoted in *Contingent Magazine*, "How Allison Horrocks Does History."

Documentary Filmmaker

25. Gus Mollasis, "Scenes from an Interview: Filmmaker Rory Kennedy," *Sarasota Scene*, 2021. https://scenesarasota.com.
26. Quoted in Mollasis, "Scenes from an Interview."

27. Shannon Walsh, "Skills, Desires, and Dispositions of a Documentary Filmmaker," *POV Magazine*, December 15, 2023. https://povmagazine.com.
28. Walsh, "Skills, Desires, and Dispositions of a Documentary Filmmaker."

Librarian

29. American Library Association, "Become a Librarian." www.ala.org.
30. Quoted in Cara Giaimo, "A Day in the Life of a Rock 'n' Roll Librarian," Atlas Obscura, November 6, 2017. www.atlasobscura.com.
31. Bureau of Labor Statistics, "How to Become a Librarian or Library Media Specialist," April 17, 2024. www.bls.gov.
32. Quoted in Adrianna Rebolini, "Here's What It's Really like to Be a Librarian," BuzzFeed News, November 17, 2018. www.buzzfeednews.com.

Interview with a Librarian

Melissa Cavill is a circulation supervisor at the Cotuit Library in Cotuit, Massachusetts. She has worked in libraries for over twenty years. She answered questions about her career by email.

Q: Why did you become a librarian?
A: When I started community college right after high school the library was hiring students, so I thought I'd give it a try. It didn't take long for me to realize that library work was my calling. My goal was to become a circulation supervisor after I finished my bachelor's degree in library science. I decided when I was younger to stay in the circulation department of the library, instead of moving to another department or becoming a director. I really enjoy working in circulation because it's a nice mix of being hands on with the library materials and interacting with people.

Q: Can you describe your typical workday?
A: My typical workday starts with the opening of the library. After I get everything opened, I print a paging list and pull the items that patrons requested. Those items either go into a bin to be sent out in delivery or onto our hold shelf. We receive a daily delivery of incoming items that need to be processed. While all this is happening, I field phone calls and in-person patrons who need help. In the afternoon I usually shelve books that need to be put away. I also have other tasks I work on like cataloging periodicals, cataloging our A/V [audiovisual] materials and processing our ILL (inter-library loan) requests. Before I know it it's time to start our closing procedures and go home. This is just a brief outline of what I do. In all honesty there's much more that goes into library work than people realize. One moment I could

be changing a light bulb, unclogging a toilet or setting up the projector for a program. I never know what I might be doing next and that makes it great fun!

Q: What do you like most about your job?
A: The thing I love most about my job is helping people. I have a heart for service, and I find library work very rewarding in that respect. I also love working with books and other library materials. From ordering, cataloging, processing and weeding I enjoy the whole cycle of collection development. I also like shelving books. I have a knack for organization, and I find it very satisfying to put things back in order. Librarians are above all information professionals, so you must like researching too.

Q: What do you like least about your job?
A: There's not much I don't like about my job. Some of the harder moments for me are dealing with difficult people or situations. I don't handle conflict very well, so I've had to learn how to navigate the more challenging encounters. Some examples are disagreements on library policies, asking for payment for lost or damaged items and medical emergencies. The library I work for is a small village library. I think because of our small size we don't have the same problems that libraries serving a larger population might have. Or at least the tough situations don't come up as often here.

Q: What personal qualities do you find most valuable for this type of work?
A: To do most library work I think you have to have a friendly, caring and outgoing personality. It's also helpful if you're organized, punctual and tech savvy. If you're more introverted, you could find a position with less public exposure like cataloging and acquisitions.

Q: What advice do you have for students who might be interested in this kind of career?

A: My advice for students who might be interested in library work is to volunteer at your local library. That would give you a good idea of what the job entails and what department you might like to work in. Also interviewing and/or shadowing a librarian for a day would be helpful. I think if anyone is interested in library work, they should go for it. It's such a rewarding and fun profession. I honestly love going to work every day and feel grateful for my career.

Other Jobs If You Like History

Anthropologist
Corporate historian
Editor of historical documents
Genealogist
High school history teacher
High school social studies teacher
Historian
Historical consultant or contractor
Historical preservationist
Historical reenactor
Historical researcher
Historical writer
History professor
History tutor
Journalist
Lecturer in art history
Museum curator
Museum educator
Political scientist
Tour guide

Editor's note: The online *Occupational Outlook Handbook* of the US Department of Labor's Bureau of Labor Statistics is an excellent source of information on jobs in hundreds of career fields, including many of those listed here. The *Occupational Outlook Handbook* may be accessed online at www.bls.gov/ooh.

Index

Note: Boldface page numbers indicate illustrations.

American Alliance of Museums (AAM), 28
American Historical Association (AHA), 21
American Library Association (ALA), 46, 52
Archaeological Institute of America (AIA), 14
archaeologist, **11**
   education/training requirements, 7, 10
   employers of, 12
   future job outlook, 7, 13–14
   information on, 14
   role of, 7–8
   salary/earnings, 7, 12–13
   skills/personal qualities, 7, 11–12
   typical workday, 8–10
   working conditions, 12
   work settings, 7
archivist, 4
   See also museum archivist
Association of National Park Rangers (ANPR), 36

Berlin, Andrea M., 9, 13–14
Brown, Lauren S., 17, 19

Bureau of Labor Statistics (BLS), 60
   on archaeologist, 12–13
   on documentary filmmaker, 44
   on history teacher, 20–21
   on librarian, 50, 51, 51–52
   on museum archivist, 27
   on park ranger, 32
Burns, Ken, 40

CareerOneStop (website), 27
Cavill, Melissa, 57–59
Council on Library & Information Resources (CLIR), 53

documentary filmmaker, **43**
   education/training requirements, 38, 41
   employers of, 43–44
   future job outlook, 38
   information on, 45
   role of, 38–39
   salary/earnings, 38, 43–44
   skills/personal qualities, 38, 41–42
   typical workday, 39–40
   working conditions, 42–43
   work settings, 38

Frearson, Charlotte, 7–8

Ganz, Michelle, 22, 28
Gerardin, Lisa, 33
Ghosts of Abu Ghraib (documentary), 39
Gig Is Up, The (documentary), 42

history
  other jobs in, 60
  study of, 4, 16
history teacher
  choosing college/courses for, 16
  education/training requirements, 15, 18
  employers of, 20
  future job outlook, 15, 21
  information on, 21
  role of, 15–17
  salary/earnings, 15, 20
  skills/personal qualities, 15, 18–20
  typical workday, 17
  working conditions, 20
  work settings, 15
Horrocks, Allison, 31–32

Illusions of Control (documentary), 42
International Council on Archives (ICA), 29
International Documentary Association (IDA), 45

Kennedy, Rory, 39

Lefae, Jones, 13
librarian, **51**
  education/training requirements, 46, 49
  employers of, 50
  future job outlook, 46, 51–52
  information on, 52–53
  interview with, 57–59
  role of, 46–47
  salary/earnings, 46, 51
  skills/personal qualities, 46, 49–50
  typical workday, 47–49
  work settings, 46, 50

Martin, Jane, 50
Matro, Katharina, 15–16
Maxwell, Sharon, 23, 25, 28
Mollasis, Gus, 39
museum archivist, **26**
  education/training requirements, 22, 24–25
  employers of, 27
  future job outlook, 22, 27–28
  information on, 28–29
  role of, 22–23
  salary/earnings, 22, 27
  skills/personal qualities, 22, 25–26
  typical workday, 23–24
  working conditions, 26–27
  work settings, 22

National Council for History Education (NCHE), 21
National Council for the Social Studies (NCSS), 21
National Parks Traveler (website), 30–31, 36
National Recreation and Park Association (NRPA), 37
Neusius, Sarah W., 8

Occupational Outlook Handbook (Bureau of Labor Statistics), 60

Parent, Jenn, 23, 24
Park Law Enforcement Association (PLEA), 37
park ranger, **35**
   education/training requirements, 30, 32–33
   employers of, 34
   future job outlook, 30, 35–36
   information on, 36–37
   role of, 30–31
   salary/earnings, 30, 34–35
   skills/personal qualities, 30, 33–34
   typical workday, 31–32
   working conditions, 34
   work settings, 30

Randolph, Stephanie, 16–17, 20
researcher, 4

Society for American Archaeology (SAA), 14
Society for Historical Archaeology (SHA), 14
Society of American Archivists (SAA), 29
Special Libraries Association (SLA), 53
Spencer, Chuck, 8, 10
Stearns, Peter N., 4
Sundance Institute Documentary Film Program (DFP), 45
Synanon Fix, The (documentary), 39

Teacher.org, 18–19

University of Wisconsin–Madison, 6

Verma, Anubha, 25

Walsh, Shannon, 42, 44
Working Films, 45

Picture Credits

Cover: Microgen/Shutterstock

11: Reinhard Dirscherl/Alamy Stock Photo
26: Associated Press
35: Jeffrey Isaac Greenberg 3+/Alamy Stock Photo
43: Ros Drinkwater/Alamy Stock Photo
51: Drazen Zigic/Shutterstock

About the Author

Historian and award-winning author Don Nardo has written numerous volumes about the ancient world and is a member of the Association of Ancient Historians. In addition, he has turned out a number of books about American history, including studies of several of the country's wars and the founding fathers and their writings. Nardo, who also composes and arranges orchestral music, lives with his wife, Christine, in Massachusetts.